P9-DBT-151

Elizabeth Blackwell

Elizabeth Blackwell

FIRST WOMAN PHYSICIAN

TRISTAN BOYER BINNS

FRANKLIN WATTS
A Division of Scholastic Inc.
New York Toronto London Auckland Sydney
Mexico City New Delhi Hong Kong
Danbury, Connecticut

For my mother, my grandmothers, and all the women who encouraged my ambitions and never questioned my abilities.

ACKNOWLEDGMENTS

The Author would like to thank the following for permission to reproduce material:

In Chapter Three, *Punch* magazine for the poem about Elizabeth Blackwell, originally published in 1849.

Most of the quotations in Elizabeth Blackwell's own words come from her 1895 autobiography, *Pioneer Work in Opening the Medical Profession to Women.*

Photographs © 2005: akg-Images, London: 20 (Archiv Für Kunst Und Geschichte, London), 22; Alex Peck Medical Antiques: back cover; AP/Wide World Photos: cover; Brown Brothers: 13, 31, 41, 50, 70; Corbis Images: 12, 18, 35, 59, 65, 72 (Bettmann), 82 (Hulton-Deutsch Collection), 75 (Medford Historical Society Collection), 30, 48, 74; Geneva Historical Society: 28, 99; Glasgow University: 33; Hobart & William Smith College Archives: 2, 64 top, 89, 92; Hulton|Archive/Getty Images: 61 (MPI), 6 (Humphrey Spender); Library of Congress: 25 (Blackwell Family Papers), 76; Mary Evans Picture Library: 9, 64; National Library of Medicine: 37; North Wind Picture Archives: 15; PhotoEdit/Tony Freeman: 97; PictureHistory.com: 52; Time Life Pictures/Getty Images: 96.

Library of Congress Cataloging-in-Publication Data

Binns, Tristan Boyer,
   Elizabeth Blackwell : first woman physician / Tristan Boyer Binns.
     p. cm. — (Great life stories.)
   Includes bibliographical references and index.
   ISBN 0-531-12402-9
   1. Blackwell, Elizabeth, 1821–1910—Juvenile literature. 2. Women physicians—United States—Biography—Juvenile literature. 3. Women physicians—England—Biography—Juvenile literature. I. Title. II. Series.
   R154.B623B54 2005
   610'.92—dc22

                                 2004025233

Contents

Elizabeth was born near Bristol, which has been a busy seaport for centuries.

ONE

A Bright Beginning

On February 3, 1821, a baby girl was born in the village of Counterslip, near the prosperous city of Bristol in the west of England. Her parents, Samuel and Hannah Blackwell, named her Elizabeth. They watched over her carefully. She had two older sisters, Anna and Marian, but an older brother had died as a baby. Elizabeth Blackwell is remembered today for all her hard-won victories, but her first struggle was to grow strong enough to live. Stubborn and determined to succeed even as a newborn baby, Elizabeth joined the Blackwell family in her own true style.

Elizabeth Blackwell became the first woman to graduate from medical school in the United States. She was a fierce and dedicated social reformer, believing strongly in the rights of human beings to be the best they could, no matter their gender or color. She did many great things. She became the first woman medical doctor, or M.D., in the United States. She opened the first women-run hospital and was the first woman to appear on the British Medical Register.

THE UNUSUAL BLACKWELLS

From her family, Elizabeth Blackwell learned to feel responsible for how other people were treated. This unusual family also helped her to grow confident in her own ability to succeed. Elizabeth's father, Samuel Blackwell, was a successful businessman in Bristol. He ran a sugar refinery, a factory that turns sugarcane into sugar crystals to be used in food. He had strong moral beliefs, most of which were not shared by many other British people of his time. He believed in liberal politics, wanting the government to help people who couldn't help themselves. He thought that owning slaves was one of the most cruel things people could do. He spoke out against slavery as an abolitionist. He struggled with a personal problem. While he hated slavery, slave labor was used on the plantations he bought his sugarcane from.

Everyone in England was supposed to believe in the state religion, a form of Christianity called Church of England, or Anglicanism. Samuel and Hannah Blackwell didn't believe in it. They were Congregational Christians who believed very strongly in being responsible for their own actions and having high moral standards.

Because the Blackwells were Congregationalists, they were called Dissenters. Dissenters were people who didn't believe in the Church of England. At the time this made their lives difficult. Dissenters couldn't be doctors, lawyers, professors, or top politicians. They also couldn't attend most schools or any universities. This meant that the Blackwell children were taught by tutors in their home and learned together instead of going to school.

Samuel and Hannah were also unusual in the way they regarded women. They thought women and men were equals. At home this meant

Men and Women

At the time, most people believed that men and women were entirely different. Women were thought to have weaker bodies but stronger morals than men. Women were supposed to look after their homes and families. Men were supposed to go out into the world to earn money, to provide for and protect their families. This meant that most girls were taught household skills and refined subjects, such as painting, music, and French. Only boys learned practical subjects, such as math, Latin, and geography.

their children were educated in the same way. They all learned the same subjects and received an excellent basic education.

Beyond the classroom, the Blackwells talked about important subjects all the time. The children's questions and thoughts were respected and taken seriously in their home. Their parents liked hearing them work on and solve problems. They encouraged this kind of investigation. Elizabeth thrived in this environment. She wanted her work to be a challenge.

MOVING HOME

When Elizabeth was about three years old, the family moved to a house in Bristol, at 1 Wilson Street. The house was pleasant and large. It was next to Samuel's sugar refinery. The strong smell of cooking sugarcane filled the air. They had a big household, with servants to help cook, clean, and look after the babies and help with the children. The older children had a governess who helped teach them and took them for long walks around Bristol. Most parents didn't want their daughters to get much exercise, especially outdoors. The Blackwells believed that fresh air and exercise helped keep people healthy, even girls.

The Blackwells lived there until about 1829, when they needed more space. They moved to Nelson Street, next to Samuel's new sugar refinery. The previous one had burned down, as sugar refineries often did. They also rented a country house in nearby Olveston each summer.

In August 1832, Samuel decided to move the whole family to the United States. Cholera and other diseases such as typhoid and influenza kept sweeping through British cities in waves. England kept experiencing tough economic times during which jobs and money became scarce. Riots led by angry workers erupted. Many people were afraid for their health, doubted their ability to earn money to support their families, and were unsure of the future. During the 1800s, hundreds of thousands of people left Britain for the United States, hoping for a better life. Samuel had suffered some large business losses and hoped that the United States would be a place where his business would flourish. He also thought that Americans were more tolerant of unusual beliefs and would welcome his family.

Three unmarried aunts, the governess, and the babies' nurse sailed along with Samuel and Hannah and their eight children on the *Cosmo*. The trip to New York took seven weeks and three days, described by Anna Blackwell as "a floating hell." The ship offered fairly good accomodations for people like the Blackwells, who could pay for them. Poorer families traveled in terrible conditions. Cholera broke out on the ship, as it had in Bristol before they left. Cholera is a disease transmitted through dirty water and sewage that thrives in crowded, filthy places, such as

Life in England in the 1800s

English society was split into social classes. The upper class owned most of the land and had most of the power and money. The middle class had skilled jobs and owned businesses, but were at the mercy of economic hard times. The working class owned little and worked very hard for very little pay. People from the higher classes usually lived longer than working-class people did.

immigrant ships. No one understood this then, but everyone feared the disease, since many people who got it died.

In New York, Samuel worked to get his business going again. The family welcomed its last baby, George Washington Blackwell. There were nine surviving children altogether. The children started going to school and making friends. They explored New York with a great deal of freedom. They joined abolitionist groups and all worked hard to end slavery. Samuel became friends with important abolitionists. There are stories about how the Blackwell family hid escaped slaves. The Blackwells were in danger when anti-abolitionists rioted in New York in the mid-1830s. In 1833, all slaves in the British Empire were freed, but it would be three more decades before slaves in the United States were free. Samuel kept trying to resolve his personal problem with slave-grown sugarcane, even trying to take the sugar out of beets. Nothing worked.

In about 1835, the Blackwells moved across the Hudson River to Paulus Hook, now called Jersey City. In 1835, fires in New York burned

The Blackwells were active in the abolitionist movement. Here a group of protesters march through New York City to voice their opposition to slavery.

for three days and destroyed forty blocks of the city, which was very small at the time. Even though the Blackwell's refinery was not burned, Samuel couldn't get fire insurance any longer. He spent a lot of time and energy sleeping at the refinery in Manhattan, making sure it didn't catch fire. Sadly, it did in September 1836. He built another one, but was so short of money six months later that he had to sell it. During the economic depression of 1837, the family grew poorer. Finally, in May 1838, the Blackwells made another big move, this time to the American West.

MOVING WEST

There was only one sugar refinery in Cincinnati, which was a small, young city in 1838. Samuel took the family there, with no servants and just Aunt Mary this time. Anna and Marian stayed in the East, where they had teaching jobs. The journey was tiring and hard and took nine days by railroad, canal boat, and steamboat. When they arrived, they

After all their troubles in New York, the Blackwell family hoped to have a better life in Cincinnati.

found a home. Samuel started his business even though he was worn out. Before he had a chance to succeed, he grew ill. No one is sure what illness he actually had.

Samuel had always been Elizabeth's greatest hero. He gave her confidence and opportunities, and they had fun together. Now she hovered around him with the rest of the family as his illness got worse. The doctors tried all cures they knew, mostly using chemicals to make him vomit and have diarrhea. They thought this would drive the illness out of his body. Samuel weakened and then died on August 7, 1838. Elizabeth wrote, "I felt as if all hope & joy were gone, & nought was left but to die also. . . . I seemed alone in the world."

Two days later the rest of the family faced the bad news that they had no money and plenty of debts. They decided to set up a school in their home. When Anna and Marian arrived from the East, they would teach with Elizabeth and Aunt Mary. Hannah would run the domestic side of the Cincinnati English and French Academy for Young Ladies, looking after the students who lived with them. The school was a success because of the family's skillful teaching and the fearless work they did to find pupils. They advertised and knocked on doors all over the city. They had barely started the school when Aunt Mary suddenly died in September of the same illness Samuel had.

Now there were the three oldest daughters teaching, Hannah looking after the school and the family, the two oldest boys at fifteen and thirteen working as clerks, and four small children living at home. Over the next few years the family did well, working hard and paying off their debts. By 1842, the younger brothers were old enough to work outside the home. This was very helpful because the academy had lost all its pupils during another economic depression and was forced to close. The family started taking in boarders to earn money.

One day in spring 1844, Elizabeth was asked to take a new job as the only teacher in a new girls' school in Henderson, Kentucky. She was offered a large enough salary that refusing seemed impossible. Henderson

The Antislavery Movement

Since their foundings, many farms and plantations in the United States relied on slave labor. Because of the landscape and climate, the biggest farms were located in the South. They used the most slave labor. By 1820, people, especially Northerners, started wanting to free the slaves. The American Anti-Slavery Society was founded in Philadelphia in 1833. Abolitionists would help runaway slaves escape through the Northern states to freedom in Canada. Slavery would be one of the issues that led to the Civil War in 1861. All slaves were finally freed when the war ended in 1865.

was in the far west of Kentucky, itself a slave state. The journey there was difficult and took almost four days. Henderson was a small, muddy country town. Most of the white people who lived there farmed tobacco. They had black slaves to do the hard work. Elizabeth had met slaves before, but they were runaways trying to make better lives for themselves in the North. She had a difficult time seeing the realities of slavery up close. The slaves were not allowed to have much money. They seldom had new clothes or even clothes in good condition. Slaves were not allowed to receive educations. Their masters were often cruel, not usually whipping or beating their slaves, but simply never thinking of them as people. A young slave girl was once placed between Elizabeth and a fire that was burning too hot, as if the slave were a wooden screen instead of a live person. According to Elizabeth, the white women in Henderson were usually scared of slaves. They seldom went out into the lovely countryside. Most lived very dull lives with only religious worship and gossip-filled social visits to fill their time.

Despite having a full class of twenty-one girls and doing private teaching on the side, Elizabeth got bored by the lack of mental stimulation. Her family always had such interesting arguments, outings, and visitors. Her moral sense grew sicker at the state of the society in which she was living. She didn't feel able to challenge her hosts on the issue of slavery because she was afraid they would shut her out entirely. She wrote in a letter home,

> I dislike slavery more and more everyday; I suppose I see it here in
> its mildest form. . . . But to live in the midst of beings degraded to
> the utmost in body and mind, drudging on from earliest morning to

latest night, . . . scolded at all day long, blamed unjustly, and without spirit enough to reply, with no consideration in any way for their feelings, with no hope for the future, smelling horribly . . . —to live in their midst, utterly unable to help them, is to me dreadful . . .

After nearly six months in Henderson, Elizabeth gave up her post and went home.

In Cincinnati, Elizabeth Blackwell liked studying and attending events, but wanted to have some purpose to her life.

A Hard Challenge

Before she got home, Elizabeth Blackwell's family had moved to a suburb of Cincinnati called Walnut Hills. Once there, Blackwell made friends with Harriet Beecher Stowe, who later wrote the popular antislavery novel *Uncle Tom's Cabin*. The family was doing well, and Blackwell didn't need to earn money. She occupied her time by studying German, music, and metaphysics. Metaphysics is a way of thinking about the world. She went to writing groups and dinner parties. She enjoyed herself, but felt frustrated by lack of any serious goal.

Blackwell also had to face the problems of marriage. She was twenty-three years old and considered too old to be unmarried. The difficulty was not a lack of attraction to men. As she herself puts it, "I never remember the time from my first adoration, at seven years old, . . . when I had not suffered more or less from the common malady—falling in love." The problem was marriage itself. At the time, when a woman married, she lost her rights to her property, income, and body. She had no rights to her own children. Essentially, she stopped being a separate person and was absorbed into her husband in the eyes of the law. Blackwell was not willing to let this happen to her. She never met a man she thought could face down these laws and customs to let her live her own life as part of a married couple.

One of Blackwell's friends was dying, probably of cancer of the uterus. Women at the time were taught to be incredibly modest about

Women Doctors

During the 1600s and 1700s, it didn't matter if you were male or female if you could help the sick in North America. Doctors qualified by serving as apprentices. This meant they learned from other doctors, not in medical schools. Until the late 1700s, most babies were delivered by women called midwives. Then male doctors replaced midwives, and male medical schools intended only for men replaced apprenticeships. Women were thought too delicate, too modest, and not smart enough to be doctors. In the mid-1800s, a doctor named Charles Meigs said, "[women's heads are] almost too small for intellect, but just big enough for love."

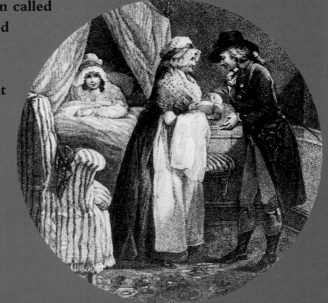

their bodies. Any discussion of how a body worked, or even acknowl-edging its parts, was horrifying to a proper lady. Men were not supposed to see a woman's body naked. Because all doctors were men, this made many ladies feel that talking with or being examined by a doctor was worse than the illness itself. Blackwell's dying friend told her, "You are fond of study, have health and leisure; why not study medicine? If I could have been treated by a lady doctor, my worst sufferings would have been spared me."

At first Blackwell thought becoming a doctor was an awful idea, because bodies and illness disgusted her. Over time, however, the idea took hold. The hard work and study involved sounded good to her. She liked the personal challenge of overcoming her squeamishness. She also wrote in her journal, "I felt more determined than ever to become a physician, and thus place a strong barrier between me and all ordinary marriage."

THE SEARCH FOR A PLACE

Over the next few months Blackwell wrote to physicians she knew about becoming a doctor. She also spoke with her family and friends about it. All her friends and advisors told her it was impossible. Women couldn't attend medical school, couldn't get training, couldn't set up a practice. As she wrote,

> This verdict, however, no matter from how great an authority, was rather an encouragement than otherwise to a young and active per-son who needed an absorbing occupation. If an idea, I reasoned,

Becoming a Doctor

In the 1840s, the process of becoming a doctor was very different than it is today. There were few state requirements and little licensing, as there is now. All medical students were men. Usually, a student spent three years studying with a doctor. Then he went to medical school for two years, which was expensive. The first school year lasted from October to January. Then the student had to work in a hospital to gain experience. The next school year also lasted from October to January, and repeated the same courses from the first year. After he graduated with an M.D., a new doctor worked to gain more experience before setting up his own practice.

were really a valuable one, there must be some way of realising it. The idea of winning a doctor's degree gradually assumed the aspect of a great moral struggle, and the moral fight possessed immense attraction for me.

Blackwell kept exploring opportunities to study, and found the Reverend John Dickson in Asheville, North Carolina. He had been a doctor and would help her begin studies. She would teach music in his school to save money for medical school. It took eleven days for her two brothers to drive Blackwell to Asheville in June 1845, and when they left, she once again felt very alone. She describes her first night there as being full of dread and doubt. Then she says she had a spiritual vision, after which "All doubt as to my future, all hesitation as to the rightfulness of my purpose, left me, and never in afterlife returned. I *knew* that, however insignificant my individual effort might be, it was in a right direction, and in accordance with the great providential ordering of our race's progress."

In December 1845, Reverend Dickson closed his school. In January Blackwell traveled to Charleston, South Carolina. She taught at a local boarding school for the next sixteen months. She also studied medicine with Reverend Dickson's brother, Dr. Samuel H. Dickson. Her two years living in these slave states again forced her to confront the horrors of slavery. By the summer of 1847, she felt ready to apply to medical schools.

The center of medical study in the United States at the time was Philadelphia. Blackwell went there. She started writing to and meeting with doctors and colleges. She lived with a doctor and his family and studied anatomy with another doctor for the first time. She learned how the human body is built by dissecting dead bodies. She found this work fascinating.

Between May and October, Blackwell applied to about twenty-nine medical schools and was rejected by all but two. Most simply said women must not be doctors, as the idea was too unnatural. Many said she should study to be a nurse instead. One said that women doctors would be too successful and steal too many patients away from male doctors. One medical-school dean wrote, "You cannot expect us to furnish you with a stick to break our heads with." Several doctors suggested that she travel to Paris, the center of medical study in Europe, to study. Women could disguise themselves as men and atttend lectures there but couldn't get degrees. Blackwell thought this was a terrible idea. She didn't just want the medical knowledge. She meant to become a fully qualified M.D.

ATTENDING GENEVA MEDICAL COLLEGE

Finally, after the term had begun, Geneva Medical College in upstate New York agreed to admit Elizabeth Blackwell. A famous doctor had recommended her, and the school's teachers didn't want to upset him. They decided to let the students vote on letting a woman student into the school. The students, a rowdy bunch of men, thought it was a great joke. They all agreed to let Blackwell into Geneva, either because they thought the teachers were making the whole thing up, or because they thought it would embarrass the teachers to have a woman there. Either way, Blackwell had her chance and set off for Geneva on November 4.

She was also accepted by Castleton Medical College in Vermont, but chose not to attend.

After arriving in Geneva and finding a room in a boardinghouse, Blackwell officially enrolled at Geneva Medical College. Her room was a three-minute walk from school. When her fellow boarders found out she was studying medicine, they shunned her. She was to find that most of the townspeople thought she was either a bad woman or insane. She wrote, "The ladies stopped to stare at me, as at a curious animal." She never felt comfortable in town and hated being singled out. She also hated the press reports of her arrival at school. The *Boston Medical Journal* wrote, "She is a pretty little specimen of the feminine gender." The *Baltimore Sun* wrote, "She should confine her practice, when admitted, to diseases of the heart." The *Sun* meant love and family, not heart disease.

Before Blackwell arrived, lectures were so wild that students often could not hear the professors. Townspeople had even threatened to close the college because of the noise. On November 8, Blackwell went

After much effort, Blackwell was admitted to Geneva Medical College. This is the letter of acceptance she received from the school.

to her first lecture as student number 130. A fellow student, Dr. Stephen Smith, wrote what it was like.

> . . . a lady entered the lecture-room with the professor; she was quite small of stature, plainly dressed, appeared diffident and retiring but had a firm and determined expression of face. Her entrance into that . . . confusion acted like magic upon every student. Each hurriedly sought his seat, and the most absolute silence prevailed. For the first time a lecture was given without the slightest interruption, and every word could be heard. . . . A more orderly class of medical students was never seen than this, and it continued to be to the close of the term.

Regular, Irregular, and Women Doctors

In the mid-1800s, the term "woman doctor" usually meant an abortionist. "Regular" doctors went to medical school and had degrees. Their treatments were usually designed to try and drive a disease out of the body. They bled the patient, or purged him, making him vomit or have diarrhea. It often didn't work. Until Elizabeth Blackwell was awarded her degree, no woman was a "regular" doctor. Because "regular" treatment was so awful, many people sought treatment from "irregular" doctors. "Irregular" doctors used treatments such as hypnotism, homeopathy, cold-water cures, and herbal medicine. Many women studied and practiced as "irregular" doctors, especially using herbal and homeopathic treatments.

Blackwell wrote, "[I] certainly have no reason to complain of medical students, for though they eye me curiously, it is also in a very friendly manner. . . . I sometimes think I'm too much disciplined, but it is certainly necessary for the position I occupy. I believe the professors don't exactly know in what species of the human family to place me, and the students are a little bewildered." As the students got used to her, they started to treat her like an older sister. They were kind and helpful and behaved like gentlemen. Although the big college building confused her at first, she was soon more happy there than anywhere else in Geneva.

Dr. James Webster, the anatomy professor, was Blackwell's friend and supporter. He had a great sense of humor. He was afraid that his rude jokes would shock her when they began studying the anatomy of the reproductive system. He asked her not to come to those lectures and dissections. Blackwell protested, saying that she would not be embarrassed, since what was being taught was simply part of the human body. If he would be embarrassed, she would willingly hide in the back of the room so he could ignore her. He read her letter to the class and they agreed she should be allowed to attend. Webster admitted he was wrong, and Blackwell never faced being excluded from a class again.

The first actual lecture about reproduction was difficult. Blackwell wrote, "Some of the students blushed, some were hysterical, not one could keep in a smile. . . . My delicacy was certainly shocked . . . but I sat in grave indifference, though the effort made my heart palpitate most painfully."

Dr. Charles Alfred Lee, the dean, said to Blackwell soon after she started, "I'll venture to say in ten years' time one-third the classes in our college will consist of women. After the precedent you will have established, people's eyes will be opened."

At Geneva Medical College, Blackwell found some support from fellow students and professors.

THREE

Gaining Experience

By the time the term ended in January, Elizabeth Blackwell was sorry to leave the school. She had none of the letters of recommendation she had been promised to help her find work during the break. While trying to find a job, she published some stories and taught music lessons to earn money. She decided she should work at the Philadelphia Almshouse and Hospital, also called Blockley, where sick and poor people went to be treated. About two thousand people were housed there. There was never enough money or staff to care for them properly. Blackwell had a hard time getting in. Once she was there she found the chief physician, Dr. Benedict, very kind and helpful. She admired his way with patients, and how he seemed to soothe them with his sympathy.

Blackwell worked at Blockley from March to September. The resident doctors were difficult to deal with. She wrote, "When I walked into the wards they walked out." They took patients' case notes with them when they left, so Blackwell had to rediagnose the patients she saw. Patients would come and stare through the keyhole in her office door to see the amazing sight of a woman doctor working.

An outbreak of typhus came to the country on the ships crowded with Irish immigrants during the summer of 1848. There were not enough beds for the sick. Many patients were crowded into hallways and slept in beds on the floors. Blackwell was fascinated and appalled by typhus, and wrote her graduation thesis on it. The thesis was very well thought of. By the time Blackwell left Blockley, she felt comfortable there too. It was another different and hostile environment that she had conquered and made her own.

At Blockley, the resident doctors gave Blackwell a hard time and the patients were fascinated by the sight of a woman doctor.

Contagious Diseases

During the 1800s, most cities had few sources of clean water and hardly any proper sewers. Most working people didn't eat nutritious food. They either couldn't afford it, or the food they bought had germs in it. This made them weak and unable to fight off infections. Often, the water used for drinking and washing was polluted with the feces of people ill with cholera or typhoid. In cities and other crowded places, diseases spread quickly and killed tens of thousands. Immigrant ships were plagued with disease for the same reasons. In England in 1839, eight out of every nine people died from diseases, not old age or accidents.

Blackwell's last term at Geneva went well. She fell back into the routine of medical school easily. She even took part in campus debates over politics, mostly about slavery. She felt secure enough to say she was firmly against slavery. Her brother Howard was heading for England at the age of seventeen. He stopped to see her on the way around Christmas. She was delighted to see him. He brought her bad news about her family's finances, which worried her.

In spite of feeling like she belonged at Geneva, the problem of what life and work would be like when she graduated bothered her. In January, she visited a blind girl left alone to recover in a hotel after an operation. Blackwell felt pity at her situation. The girl was alone yet very friendly and hopeful. She wrote, "Such are the women I long to surround with my stronger arm. Alas! How almost hopeless does the task seem!"

GRADUATING FROM SCHOOL

At the end of January, Blackwell passed her final exams. The staff debated whether they could actually award Blackwell a degree. They finally agreed to do so after Dr. Webster fought for her. The graduation ceremony was held in a Presbyterian church on January 23, 1849. The church was packed, mostly with women, to see Blackwell graduate. She wore a new black silk dress and gloves. The men marched into the church in rows, but Blackwell thought it would not be ladylike and modest to join them. She came in quietly on her brother Henry's arm after the other students, joining them as they went through the church.

All the men were given their diplomas by Dr. Hale, the president, in groups of four. Then Blackwell went up to Dr. Hale on her own. He took off his hat, stood, and gave her the diploma while telling her in Latin that she was officially a doctor. She bowed and said, "Sir, I thank you; it shall be the effort of my life, with the help of the Most High, to shed honor on my diploma." The audience applauded. Dr. Lee gave a speech and called Blackwell "the *leader* of her class . . . by her ladylike and dignified deportment [she] had proved that the strongest intellect and nerve and the most untiring perseverance were compatible with the softest attributes of feminine delicacy and grace." As she left, the students clapped, people crowded around her, and even the conservative bishop congratulated her. She left Geneva the next day, surrounded by people wishing her well.

Around the country and even in Europe, the press took notice of Blackwell's achievement. The famous *Punch* magazine from London, which specialized in commenting on current events and making fun of politicians, published a poem about her. It said she deserved "esteem and admiration."

On January 23, 1849, Elizabeth Blackwell broke new ground for women when she was the first to receive a medical degree.

Young ladies all, of every clime,
　　Especially of Britain,
Who wholly occupy your time
　　In novels or in knitting,
Whose highest skill is but to play,
　　Sing, dance, or French to clack well
Reflect on the example, pray,
　　Of excellent Miss Blackwell!

Think, if you had a brother ill,
　　A husband, or a lover,
And could prescribe the draught or pill
　　Whereby he might recover;
How much more useful this would be,
　　Oh, sister, wife, or daughter!
Than merely handing him beef-tea,
　　Gruel, or toast-and-water.

GOING TO EUROPE

After graduating, Blackwell needed more work experience before she could set up her own practice. She wanted to become a surgeon most of all. She went to Philadelphia to attend lectures and ask doctors for help. They said she should go to Paris, the center of European medical knowledge. Her cousin Kenyon was traveling back to England, so she planned to go with him in April. Blackwell had a short visit with her family in Cincinnati first. Before she left Philadelphia, she became an official U.S. citizen.

Doctors and Surgeons

In England at the beginning of the 1800s, doctors, or physicians, were at the top of the medical profession. Next came surgeons, who performed amputations and other surgery but very often killed their patients. Finally there were apothecaries, who gave advice and prepared medicines. Usually, a person would first see an apothecary to be examined, then take the notes to a physician. The physician would prescribe medicines. Later in the 1800s, surgeons gained respect when better surgical techniques and hygiene meant that fewer patients died. By 1877, the death rate from surgery was down 50 percent.

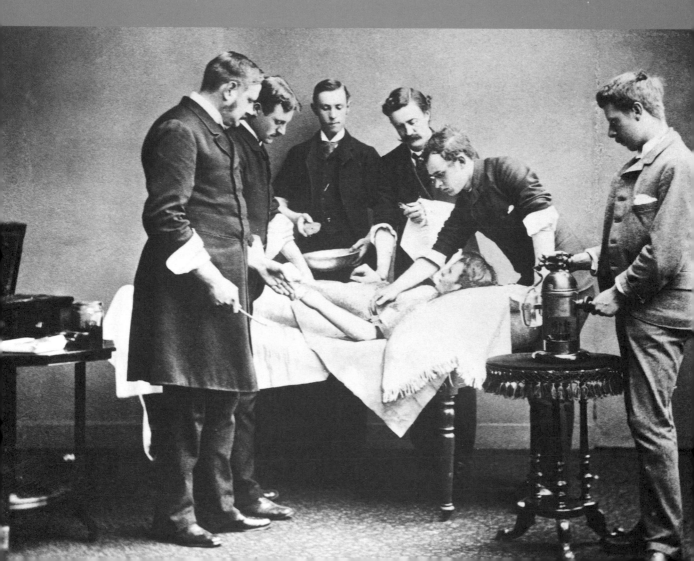

In England, she spent some time visiting relatives and seeing the sights. She paid a lot of attention to how the working people looked, comparing their health with that of U.S. workers. She thought they seemed similar and were better off than she had expected. Doctors and hospitals in Birmingham and London welcomed her. They always asked if she should be called "Doctor Blackwell," and she always said yes. She went to parties and met many people. Her three-week visit was packed full, and she enjoyed it very much.

By May 21, Blackwell had arrived in Paris. She was alone in a new city and didn't speak French fluently. After finding a boardinghouse and practicing her French with her landlady, she started to look for a hospital that would give her a job. None would have her. Her degree was not recognized, and she was scorned as a woman doctor. She felt "quite disappointed with the city." At the beginning of June, her sister Anna moved to Paris, and she felt happier. People wanted to change the way Paris was run. In June, soldiers and revolutionaries filled the streets on some days.

WORKING AT LA MATERNITÉ

The doctors Blackwell consulted with advised her to work at La Maternité. This was a large hospital where women went to give birth. Blackwell was allowed to go there for three months, but not as a doctor. She was to enter with the young French girls who had no education. They went there as apprentices to learn to be midwives. La Maternité was run very strictly. Visitors were only allowed in one big open room, the working hours were long, study groups filled most of the rest of the students' time, there wasn't much food, and students were seldom allowed off the site. All the students lived in large dormitories with no privacy, and even bath time was supervised. Blackwell entered happily, looking forward to seeing as many births there in her three months as many doctors see in a lifetime.

At the end of June, her internship began. She had a hard time adjusting to the strict routine, poor food, and lack of sleep. In spite of this, she did indeed learn very much. Her first night she helped deliver eight babies. She learned to use leeches to bleed patients, which was a popular treatment method of the time. During study groups she helped explain some of the medical information and improved her French. She had respect for the French girls there and enjoyed their company. However, she felt they were often too full of energy, as she wrote in a letter to her mother.

> You must know that our bedsteads are of iron, and placed on rollers
> so movable that a slight [push] will speed them a considerable dis-
> tance. . . . This property of these usually sober pieces of furniture is

At La Maternité, Blackwell found her internship challenging, but informative.

taken advantage of by the girls . . . the favorite freak is to place a bedstead at the end of the room and drive it with great violence down the center. The rolling noise over the brick floor is tremendous, and accompanied by a regular Babel of laughter, shouting, and jokes of every description.

Blackwell became friends with one of the intern doctors, Monsieur Blot, and gave him English lessons. At the end of her three months she decided to stay another three. Then disaster struck. On November 4, she was cleaning the eye of a baby with ophthalmia, an eye infection that caused blindness. Some of the pus flew into her own eye. By nighttime her eye was swollen. The next day she was put to bed as a patient of Monsieur Blot. She spent three weeks with both eyes swollen shut, nursed by her sister Anna and Monsieur Blot. She left La Maternité on November 26, able to see a little with her right eye but not at all with her left. Over the next six months, she could not work or read much and felt weak. A famous eye specialist in Paris finally cured her right eye by removing her infected left eye. She had a glass eye put in its place. Because surgeons need good eyesight, her dreams of becoming a surgeon were shattered.

FOUR

Struggling to Start

In 1850, Blackwell heard from one of the top hospitals in London, St. Bartholomew's. She was invited to study there, so she moved from Paris to London in October. She wrote at the time, "I was a quiet, sensible person who had acquired a small amount of medical knowledge, and who wished by patient observation and study to acquire considerably more." As she spent more time at lectures and watching doctors work, she grew less happy with the state of "regular" medical treatments. "I spend now about three or four hours each day in the wards, chiefly medical, diagnosing disease, watching the progress of cases, and accustoming my ear to the stethoscope." Blackwell spent a great deal of time researching "irregular" treatments but was not satisfied with them either. She wanted to find the best treatments for herself. She wrote to her sister Emily, who was then trying to get into medical school:

I shall commence as soon as possible building up a hospital in which I can experiment; and the very instant I feel *sure* of any improvement I shall adopt it in my practice. . . . If I were rich I would not begin private practice, but would only experiment; as, however, I am poor, I have no choice. I look forward with great interest to the time when you can aid me in these matters, for I have really no *medical friend.*

Although she found the work very interesting, Blackwell felt alone in London. She felt none of the excitement of her first visit. The smoky fog that blanketed the city made her feel ill and unhappy. One day, three young reformers, Bessie Rayner Parkes, Barbara Leigh Smith, and Anna Leigh Smith, came to visit her. They were well connected in society and also believed in improving women's chances in life. Bessie was the leader of the women's rights movement. The women became great friends, and Blackwell suddenly found herself busy with parties and social gatherings as well as work. She felt filled with energy.

Although Blackwell worked hard for the right of women to become doctors, she didn't like the way some of the women's rights campaigners thought. She didn't think supporting women should include being against men. After the first national Women's Rights Convention in Worcester, Massachusetts, in 1850, Blackwell wrote to her mother,

They show great energy, much right feeling, but not, to my judgement, a great amount of strong, clear thought. . . . I cannot sympathise fully with an anti-man movement. I have had too much kindness, aid, and just recognition from men to make such attitude of women otherwise than painful; and I think the true end of freedom may be gained better in another way.

Barbara and Anna had a cousin named Florence Nightingale. She lived with her upper-class family on a beautiful country estate. Blackwell often visited her. At the time, nursing was not considered a respectable profession. Nightingale was determined to become a nurse, but her family would not allow it. She loved talking about medicine with Blackwell and convinced her that she should concentrate on hygiene. Nightingale talked about the six D's that threaten good health: dirt, drink, diet, dampness, drafts, and drains. Blackwell wrote,

To her, chiefly, I owed the awakening to the fact that sanitation is the supreme goal of medicine, its foundation and its crown. . . . When, in later years, I entered into practice, extremely sceptical in relation to the value of drugs and ordinary medical methods, my strong faith in hygiene formed the solid ground from which I gradually built up my own methods of treatment.

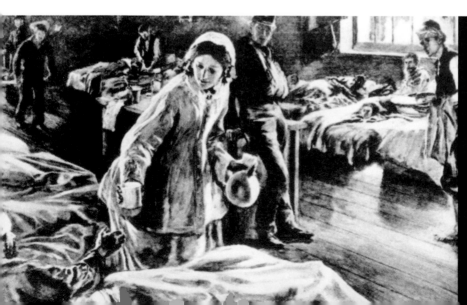

Florence Nightingale, often called the founder of modern nursing, became a friend of Blackwell's.

RETURN TO NEW YORK

By the summer of 1851, Blackwell felt ready to set up her own practice. She wanted to stay in London to practice, but missed her family. She also thought she was too poor to manage it. In Boston and Philadelphia, women's medical schools were being founded, and she felt that she should be nearby to help out. She had made plans with her sister Emily to work together when Emily earned her degree. At the end of July, she said tearful good-byes to her friends and her sister Anna, who was staying in Europe. She sailed for New York.

Blackwell wrote, "The first seven years of New York life were years of very difficult, though steady, uphill work." After being met at the dock

Scientific Nursing

Before Florence Nightingale began to reform the nursing profession, it was not thought to be a proper job for a lady. Nightingale used a mixture of compassionate care and statistical evidence to push the cause of scientific nursing. She trained nurses to act for patients, looking out for their physical needs by providing clean water, air, and surroundings. She also taught them to listen for what a patient needed emotionally. Patients needed to feel secure and well tended so they could heal quickly. She used statistics to show how badly disease affected certain groups, such as British soldiers. She drew up plans for fighting diseases with good hygiene and care. Through her efforts, nursing became a respected profession.

by her mother and sisters Marian and Ellen, Blackwell tried to find rooms to rent to set up her practice. No one would rent to a woman doctor. Finally she agreed to pay a high rent for rooms in Greenwich Village, and then faced the problem of having no patients. The *New York Tribune* published two announcements that she had opened an office, and still no patients came.

Blackwell had little money left and seemed cut off from any source of earnings. She asked to visit the wards of a nearby hospital. She applied for a job at a dispensary, a place where poor people went for medical advice and medicines. Everyone told her they didn't need or want a woman doctor. The only thing she did get was hate mail. The constant struggle wore her out, and she felt lonely. She wrote to Emily, "I understand now why this life has never been lived before. It *is* hard, with no support but a high purpose, to live against every species of social opposition. . . . I *should* like a little fun now and then."

Emily Blackwell was having no success getting accepted into medical school. Even Geneva Medical College would let no more women in, because the New York Medical Association was upset that it had awarded Blackwell's degree. Dr. Lee, the dean of Geneva, had published his speech from Elizabeth's graduation ceremony with a footnote that said he felt it was too inconvenient to have women in a medical school, so he would oppose their admission in the future.

Emily finally got accepted into Rush Medical College in Chicago, after many refusals. When she successfully finished her first year, the school would not let her back in for her second year because the doctors in Illinois complained so much. She found a place at what would become the School of Medicine of Case Western Reserve University, then called Cleveland Medical College. Emily graduated in 1854. Then she set off for Scotland, London, and Paris to gain practical experience.

At the time, women went to lecture series in much the same way as we go to the movies today. After months without any patients, Blackwell gave a series of six lectures on girls' health in March 1852. She believed that girls' bodies suffered from a lack of exercise. Girls' minds also suffered because they were not taught about their own bodies. They didn't have the vision to see themselves as strong, healthy, capable people. Their mothers could give them this gift if they themselves had the power of information. Later that year, Blackwell published her first book, a collection of her lectures. It was called *The Laws of Life with Special Reference to the Physical Education of Girls*. It was well received by other doctors.

Blackwell had a small audience for her lectures, but the women who came were very interested in what she had to say. Some were Quakers, and they started to visit Blackwell for medical advice. Soon she

Quakers and Social Reform

The Quaker religion started in England in the 1600s with a belief in the inner light of "God in every man." In the 1700s, Quakers opposed slavery and supported religious tolerance. In 1775, they were the first religious group to free all their slaves. In the 1800s, they fought for American Indians' rights, prison reform, mental hospital reform, better education for all, temperance, and women's rights. In the 1900s, they helped conscientious objectors avoid becoming soldiers and gave aid to poor people around the world.

had a small practice as a family physician. She wanted to do more and felt cut off from the kind of learning that comes from seeing a wide range of cases. After raising funds, mostly from her Quaker friends, she set up a dispensary in March 1853. For three afternoons each week, Blackwell saw patients for free at the dispensary. Soon it was a popular place for getting medical advice and advice on hygiene. Blackwell even helped the poorest families by providing small loans.

THE NEW YORK DISPENSARY

By January 1854, the New York Dispensary for Poor Women and Children was incorporated. This meant it was a success, had a board of trustees, and other doctors to consult with. All were men. Blackwell was still the only actual doctor working there. The First Annual Report of the New York Dispensary for Poor Women and Children was published on February 8, 1855, and said,

> The design of this institution is to give to poor women an opportunity of consulting physicians of their own sex. . . . The Eleventh Ward was chosen as the location for the dispensary, it being destitute of medical charity, while possessing a densely crowded poor population. . . . Over 200 poor women have received medical aid. . . . With all these patients, the necessity of cleanliness, ventilation, and judicious diet has been strongly urged, and in many cases the advice has been followed. . . . Poor women and children may be sent from any part of the city to receive the medical aid of the dispensary, it being free to all.

The dispensary was funded by gifts and paid Blackwell no salary. Her only income came from her private practice. In 1854, Blackwell got tired of not having good rooms to see her patients in. She bought a house of her own, but couldn't really afford it. She had to rent the middle floors out, and use the attic to live in and the basement for her practice. Besides the constant problem of not having enough money, Blackwell also faced threats when she went out to visit patients at night. Men thought she was a prostitute, because no other woman would be outside without a male escort at night. Even police officers were rude to her. She never gave up, always focused on her patients' needs, and carried on her work.

Keeping Clean

During most of the 1800s, people thought bad smells and night air made them sick. The idea of keeping homes and bodies clean in order to keep them healthy was revolutionary. Thousands of families lived in poverty in small apartments with no running water. Fresh air and clean water, proper disposal of waste, nutritious food, and healthy exercise for everyone seemed like impossible goals to reach. Hygiene reformers worked hard to teach people how important they were. They got governments to make laws to help. By the end of the 1800s, people understood that diseases spread through germs. Most realized how good hygiene would make life safer for everyone, not just the poor.

FIVE

New Beginnings

In the spring of 1854, Elizabeth Blackwell answered a knock at her door. Marie Zakrzewska introduced herself as a German midwife. She had been the chief midwife at the hospital of what is now the Humboldt University Medical School in Berlin. She had taught hundreds of students. She had been hired even though most of the staff objected to hiring a woman. Her boss had thought she was the best person for the job, but she was fired after he died. Immigrating to the United States seemed like the best way for her to further her career. Once there, she faced problems. She was told that doctors, not midwives, delivered babies in the United States. She was told that women should become nurses, not doctors. She felt hopeless and confused. She was given Blackwell's name and went to her for advice. Zakrzewska only spoke German, but luckily so did Blackwell.

Blackwell was very impressed by Zakrzewska's abilities. She wrote to Emily, "There is true stuff in her, and I shall do my best to bring it out. She must obtain a medical degree." Zakrzewska wrote, "She told me of her plan of founding a hospital . . . and she invited me to come and assist her. She insisted first of all I should learn English, and she offered to give me lessons twice a week and also to make efforts to enable me to enter a college to acquire the title of 'M.D.' The cordiality with which she welcomed me as a co-worker, I can never describe or forget. . . . All the days of disappointment were instantly forgotten." True to her word, Blackwell taught her English and found her a place at Cleveland Medical College in October 1854. She even found people to pay Zakrzewska's expenses. After Zakrzewska graduated, she planned to work with the Blackwell sisters for her two years' experience.

In October 1854, Elizabeth Blackwell was thirty-three years old. She was often lonely and knew she would never marry. She decided to adopt a child, thinking the companionship and help around the house would be good for her. She went to Randall's Island, where four hundred immigrant children lived in an orphanage. Blackwell chose to

Blackwell adopted a daughter from an orphanage on Randall's Island.

adopt Kitty Barry, a seven-year-old Irish girl. At first, Blackwell concentrated on teaching Kitty useful household skills. She soon grew to love and value her. Blackwell wanted Kitty to receive a good education so Blackwell enrolled her at the best girls' school in the city.

Kitty became Blackwell's faithful friend and stayed with her all her life. As she grew up she acted as Blackwell's secretary. In 1856, Blackwell wrote about how she felt adopting Kitty, "It was a dark time, and she did me good." Kitty always called Blackwell "Doctor." After a visit from a male doctor friend, Kitty said to Blackwell, "Doctor, how very odd it is to hear a *man* called Doctor!"

THE OTHER BLACKWELLS

In 1853, Elizabeth's brother, Henry Blackwell, was a successful businessman living in Cincinnati. He was still very active in the antislavery movement. He met Lucy Stone during one of her antislavery, pro-women's rights speeches. She refused to obey the laws that denied women's rights to property and legal status when they married. Like Elizabeth Blackwell, Lucy Stone felt that being an example and blazing a trail for other women to follow was important work. Henry Blackwell spent two years persuading her to marry him. He wrote, "I wish, as a husband, to *renounce* all the privileges which the *law* confers upon me, which are not strictly *mutual*. Surely *such a marriage* will not degrade you, dearest." Stone wrote, "A wife should no more take her husband's name than he should her's. My name is my identity and must not be lost." Henry agreed, and they were married in 1855. Lucy Stone was one of the first women to keep her birth name after marriage.

Lucy Stone

Since her childhood, Lucy Stone had been upset about the place of women in American society. She saw that women had few rights after marriage, couldn't vote, and were not usually educated. She was determined to change these things. Working to pay for her own education, she graduated from Oberlin College in 1847. She traveled around the country giving speeches on women's rights and the abolition of slavery. She helped organize women's rights meetings and national groups to fight for the cause. Through her inspiring words and living example, Lucy Stone helped millions of women gain rights. She died at the age of seventy-five in 1893. Her last words were "Make the world better."

In 1856, Elizabeth Blackwell's brother Samuel married Antoinette Brown. They moved to New York late that year. Soon after, Antoinette gave birth to their daughter Florence, helped by Elizabeth. Emily returned from Scotland shortly after. Briefly, Emily, Samuel, Antoinette, Lucy, Henry, Marian, Hannah, Florence, and Kitty all lived in Elizabeth's house in New York. Samuel and Antoinette's family moved to New Jersey, along with Henry and Lucy.

After Henry and Lucy's daughter Alice Stone Blackwell was born in 1857, Lucy Stone became a stay-at-home mother. When Alice was ten years old, Stone started lecturing again. She and Henry later founded the American Woman Suffrage Association, then started and edited a suffrage newspaper called *The Woman's Journal*. Alice grew up to become a leading women's rights campaigner herself. Samuel and Antoinette had five daughters, two of whom became doctors.

PLANS FOR A HOSPITAL

Both Emily and Marie Zakrzewska were back with Elizabeth by the fall of 1856. Around this time, a few women were graduating from coeducational medical schools. There were also a few new women's medical schools. Some had hospitals attached to them, so the women doctors could gain experience without facing the struggles Elizabeth and Emily had faced.

Almost every other hospital banned women doctors from working in them, but one or two had started to let women join their staff. The Blackwell sisters were worried about the ones that did. They were letting "irregular" women doctors practice, mainly graduates in homeopathy

Antoinette Brown Blackwell

A friend of Lucy Stone's at Oberlin College, Antoinette Brown stayed at Oberlin after graduating in 1847. She attended the theological seminary there, but was not awarded a degree because she was a woman. She was also not allowed to become a minister at first, but won that battle on September 15, 1853. She became the first ordained woman minister in the United States. Antoinette preached and worked for women's rights, abolition, and temperance until she was in her nineties. She died in 1921 at the age of ninety-six.

and water treatments. They were concerned that only female physicians of the highest ability who had been educated to the general standards of the time should be the ones in the public eye. They didn't want "irregular" women doctors to reverse the progress they had made toward ensuring a place for women doctors in the medical profession. Elizabeth wrote, "Experience both at the New York Hospital and at the large Bellevue Hospital, where classes of imperfectly trained women had failed to maintain their ground, proved that a special women's center was needed . . ."

The Blackwell sisters felt that the best solution was to open their own hospital especially to train women doctors. Elizabeth would be the director, Emily would be the surgeon, and Zak, as Marie Zakrzewska was known, would be the resident physician. At the time few hospitals were as large as modern ones. The women wanted to raise enough money to rent a house, adapt it to become a small hospital, and open their doors. They planned to treat both paying and non-paying patients.

Blackwell didn't think that Bellevue Hospital provided good enough training for women in medicine.

Still, the three women could only raise enough money to fund their dream through very hard work. Lectures and concerts helped raise money, but most of their funds came from craft fairs they held for the first seven years.

The New York Infirmary for Indigent Women and Children opened on Florence Nightingale's birthday, May 12, in 1857. Once again, they chose a location near many poor and immigrant people who needed their help. When they opened the infirmary on Bleecker Street in downtown New York City, they had twelve beds for patients and a maternity ward. One small bedroom was given a very large window and became the operating room. All the rooms were heated by coal fires. People who wished them well donated furniture and even medicines. As well as admitting patients to the hospital, they also saw people in the dispensary.

The doctors had to do much more than diagnose and treat patients. They also had to drill and test students, plan menus, make meals, go to fund-raising events, and do all the administrative work for the hospital. They shopped for food and medicines too. They even had to make the towels and bed linens for the patients. Zak lived in the attic with the students. Emily and Elizabeth lived in Elizabeth's house, where all three also had consulting rooms in which to see their private patients.

The first time a patient died in the infirmary there was a small riot outside caused by her relatives. They threw rocks and shouted, "Female doctors are killers!" Two friendly policemen helped calm the crowd. Later, another patient died from a burst appendix. A visiting male doctor offered to do an autopsy to show the woman's relatives how she had died. He proved the doctors could have done nothing to prevent her death. This calmed the crowd that had gathered outside the hospital.

The infirmary later published a pamphlet telling people about its goals.

First, to afford an opportunity for the medical treatment of women and children by women physicians.

Second, to give clinical instruction to women medical students.

Third, to train nurses, under female supervision.

In accordance with these aims, the resident and attending physicians have, with few exceptions been women, the consulting staff alone men.

As time went on, more students and qualified doctors came to work at the infirmary. Eight months after it opened, nurses started training

Women's Rights

In the second half of the 1800s, women struggled to gain more rights on many fronts. Many fought to gain the vote for themselves and for African Americans. As more women got educated and entered professions, they learned how to make their voices heard. Women fought to protect working children, to organize workers into unions, and to change the ways health care was provided. They worked to make the food that was sold safer to eat, to make prisons more humane, and to ban the sale of alcohol. Some of their victories were great and some were small, but all women benefited from these efforts. Women in U.S. society were growing more powerful.

there. The nursing course lasted four months and was offered free of charge. When the first two student nurses started, it became the first nursing school in the United States. It was run according to the principles Florence Nightingale had laid out.

The infirmary was a success. In its first year, the infirmary staff treated 866 patients, and had forty-eight people admitted to the hospital. The next year it served twice as many patients. By the 1920s, forty-five women doctors were on staff, and consultants both male and female were on the board. In 1927, it treated "32,000 cases in the dispensary, and over 2,500 in the hospital, of which one half were entirely free patients." The infirmary is now called the New York University Downtown Hospital. It still takes much of its philosophy from that of the Blackwell sisters who founded it. It says, "Health maintenance is the concept of providing health care in a fashion that goes beyond what traditional hospital services call for. . . . The Hospital will offer preventive services and other outreach activities. It will build on the tradition of caring for women as established by Elizabeth Blackwell, M.D."

SIX

Challenges and Successes

Everything was going well at the New York Infirmary. Blackwell's old friend from England, Barbara Leigh Smith, came to visit. She asked Blackwell to help change the medical community in England, where there were no women doctors and no special hospitals for women staffed by women. Blackwell also learned that the British were setting up a General Council of Medical Education and Registration. This group would publish a medical registry that listed the doctors allowed to practice in the United Kingdom. Doctors with degrees from foreign schools would only be allowed on the registry if they were practicing in the United Kingdom before October 1, 1858. Blackwell decided to go to

England. She would set up a small practice and get on the register. Then one woman doctor would be recognized and allowed to work in England. While she was there, she would also work to help other women break into medicine. She set off with Kitty in August of 1858.

While Elizabeth was busy planning to spread the word in England about women in health care, Emily was having problems. She was not sure she wanted to be a doctor anymore. She wrote in her private journal in July 1858, ". . . this long earnest struggle has been a mistake, that this life of a Physician is so utterly not my life." Even though this worried her very much, she didn't share her doubts about her career choice with Elizabeth.

Kitty spent the year in England first at boarding school and then with her uncle Howard and aunt Ellen. Blackwell went on to Paris to stay with her sister Anna. Anna was working as a foreign correspondent for American newspapers. Elizabeth had agreed to give lectures in England. She wrote them in Paris. There were three topics. The first was why knowing about the body would help women. The second was why knowing about medicine would help women. The third was how she had worked to allow women to have careers in medicine in the United States and how it could be done in England. While in France, Elizabeth worked with the Countess de Noailles, a wealthy woman who wanted to set up a hospital for women. She thought it should be in the countryside in England or in France. It should be somewhere where fresh air would help women recover from illnesses. The countess was a firm believer in sanitary reform and hygiene and wanted Blackwell to direct the hospital. The countess offered to set up a hospital outside New York in the countryside, and Blackwell considered the offer.

Back in England, Blackwell met with Florence Nightingale. After her exhausting work in the Crimean War, Nightingale was worn out. Blackwell was very worried about her health. They talked about the nursing school that Nightingale was planning to establish.

Medical Advances

In the second half of the 1800s, legal reforms helped clean up cities. The biggest change came from the building of better sewers. Now waste could be safely drained away. Clean water for washing and drinking became widely available. Disease rates went down. Vaccinations, such as those for smallpox and later rabies and the bubonic plague, also helped keep people from getting sick. Doctors developed new tools to help diagnose disease, such as stethoscopes and thermometers. Treatments for the sick moved away from bleeding and purging them to remove illnesses toward helping them grow strong enough to fight illnesses off.

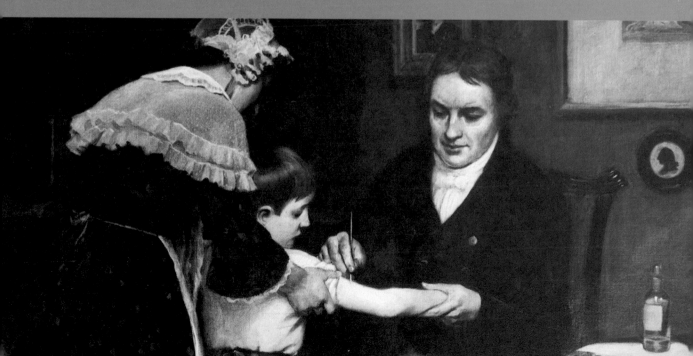

On January 1, 1859, Blackwell's name was placed on the British Medical Register. A group of doctors had looked over her qualifications and experience and agreed she was fit to practice in England. Some of the men deciding about her had known her at St. Bartholomew's Hospital. Blackwell was the first, and for seven years the only, woman on the register.

THE LECTURE TOUR

Blackwell delivered her first lecture on March 2, 1859, in London. Her old friends were there to support her, and young women such as Elizabeth Garrett attended too. Blackwell toured Manchester, Birmingham, and Liverpool, all large industrial cities. Instead of earning money, the lecture tour cost Blackwell money. However, she was excited about the amount of interest people were showing.

Blackwell wrote to a friend about the lectures in June 1859. "Mothers beg me for instruction in health. Young ladies listen eagerly to the idea of work. Three desired to become medical students. . . . Thus from many different points of view a deep interest awakens. . . . The children of the present generation will grow up accustomed to women doctors, respecting and trusting them."

Other people wanted to help women become doctors and set up a women's hospital in England. A group of them met in London and published a paper titled "Proposed Hospital for the Treatment of the Special Diseases of Women." The paper stated that women who had heard Blackwell's lectures were convinced that a hospital especially for women would help them avoid the "moral distress" they felt when examined and treated by male doctors. The supporters of the hospital were asking for people to give money to set it up. One woman had pledged a tenth of the amount needed, and it looked as if it would be difficult to collect the rest. A countrywide election was about to happen, and fund-raising stopped during the campaigning.

Blackwell wrote to Emily in April 1859: "I like working and living in England, and there is no limit to what we might accomplish here." Blackwell never considered working in England without Emily. She had written, "My sister is a noble helper, and we shall stand shoulder to shoulder through many years of active service." Not knowing of Emily's unhappiness with being a doctor, she wrote to her, "I will accept nothing that is not offered to us both, on that I am quite determined; we cannot separate in practice."

By May, Blackwell decided to return to New York. She did not have enough money to stay in Europe without earning, and it seemed like it would be years before the English hospital project would begin. She did this with regrets, as she wrote to Emily

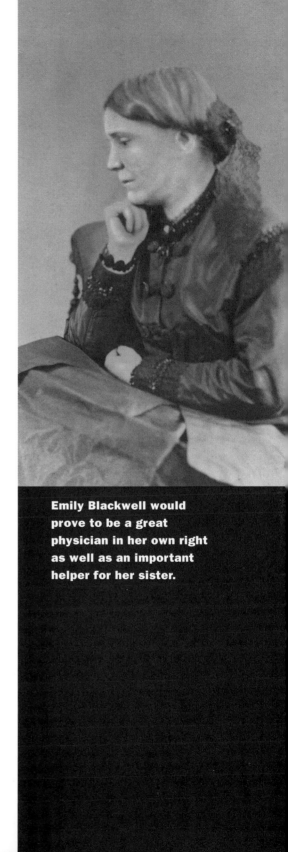

Emily Blackwell would prove to be a great physician in her own right as well as an important helper for her sister.

in July: "I cannot but think that the next ten years might be better spent in England than in America. Our work is needed, and I know not who else can do it; indeed, we seem peculiarly suited to do this work in England." Although she felt guilty about not being able to be in two places at once, she felt good that she could invite English women to be students in the New York Infirmary. In August 1859, Blackwell arrived in New York.

RETURNING TO NEW YORK

When Blackwell got home, she received some good news and some bad news. The good news was that she and her partners were successfully raising money to move the infirmary to a bigger building. Blackwell started fund-raising with new vigor to have enough to open a medical and nursing school as well.

Women's Medical Schools

In 1848, the first women's medical school in the United States was opened, the New England Female Medical College. By 1900, nineteen women's schools had opened. By 1910, only two women's medical schools were still open. The others closed because women were being admitted to coeducational medical schools instead. However, there were far fewer women studying medicine than men. Even as late as 1925, women in the United States had problems getting their internship experience after graduating. Out of 525 hospitals that offered internships, only 127 would admit women.

The bad news was from Emily. She told Elizabeth that she would keep working until she had saved enough money to live on, but her goal was to leave medicine. Emily was interested in travel and art. She would do what she had to at the infirmary but would not perform surgery anymore. She wanted to avoid as much hands-on medicine as possible. Elizabeth was very upset but knew that it would be a long time before they had earned enough money for Emily to leave. Although they were both unhappy, they agreed to keep working together, keep the infirmary going, and not talk about Emily's decision anymore.

More changes were afoot. After working in the infirmary for two years, Zak left to become a professor of obstetrics and the diseases of women and children at the New England Female Medical College in Boston. The infirmary moved to a larger building on Second Avenue in May 1860. It was big enough for the Blackwells to move in as resident physicians. There was room for more students to live in as well, and more space for patients. They created the new job of sanitary visitor, which was similar to today's social worker. This person's job was "to give simple, practical instruction to poor mothers on the management of infants and the preservation of the health of their families."

By this point, Blackwell was planning to open a women's medical school as part of the infirmary. She didn't believe that separating men and women was the best way to educate doctors. Indeed, she thought that coeducational schools were far better. Few medical schools, however, admitted women. In order to increase the number of women doctors dramatically, there would need to be special schools. Blackwell thought that their school curriculum should be more difficult than that

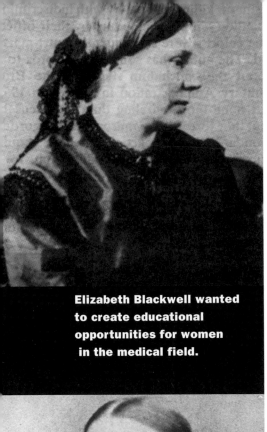

Elizabeth Blackwell wanted to create educational opportunities for women in the medical field.

Like the Blackwell sisters, Elizabeth Garrett struggled to attend medical school.

of regular medical schools. Then the graduates would show just how capable women doctors really were.

In England, one woman was struggling hard to become a doctor. She was Elizabeth Garrett, who had attended Blackwell's lectures in London. Garrett and Blackwell wrote to each other often. Garrett reported on her work and Blackwell offered advice. Garrett spent three months as a trainee nurse, then tried to become a medical student. She had no luck gaining acceptance into any medical schools, but kept studying with doctors and walking around hospitals examining patients. In January 1861, Garrett wrote, "I feel anxious to tell you how very much I enjoy the work and study, as this is to a great extent unexpected to me. As I had not any very strong interest in the subjects, and was led to choose the profession more from a strong conviction of its fitness for women than from any absorbing personal bias, I was prepared to find the first year's preparation work tedious and wearing."

Garrett was refused a place at any medical school. None of the different licensing bodies would let a woman sit for their final exams and become a licensed physician. The schools felt it would be irresponsible to give a woman a degree to become an illegal doctor. Finally, the Apothecaries' Hall agreed to give her their exam. Apothecaries were like the pharmacists of today. Even though having an apothecary license was not the same as a M.D., it was at least a start and a medical qualification. Garrett knew she might have to go to the United States to get her M.D., but she wanted to try as hard as possible to earn it in England first. That would blaze a trail for more women to follow. She lobbied colleges to admit women, but mostly failed. The harder she tried, the more she felt women should have a place in medicine. She wrote in May 1862, "I am more than ever convinced both that this special work is one which a woman may have a divine right to engage in, and that every single woman's life is both happier and more useful if she has an absorbing interest and pursuit."

Life was full of change, expansion, and new challenges for the Blackwells. It was also a time of change for the United States. Progress

The outbreak of the Civil War put plans for a women's medical school on hold.

stopped on the planned women's medical school in New York when the Civil War broke out in April 1861. The Blackwells, like most Americans, were suddenly absorbed in the war.

Causes of the Civil War

In the years before the war, the North and the South argued about how much power the states and the federal government should have. They also debated about the right to keep slaves. People took sides on both moral and economic grounds. Slave labor powered the large plantations that gave the South its wealth. There was more than $2 billion invested in slaves themselves. Smaller farms and factories in the North didn't rely on slavery. When Abraham Lincoln, who opposed the expansion of slavery into territories applying for statehood, was elected president in November 1860, Southern states started leaving the Union to join the Confederate States of America. Five months later, the Civil War began when the Confederates fired on Fort Sumter on April 12, 1861.

SEVEN

War and Opportunity

In her autobiography Blackwell wrote, "The war was essentially a rebellion by a portion of the States for the maintenance of slavery. To us, nourished from childhood on the idea of human freedom and justice, the contest became of absorbing interest. . . . We threw ourselves energetically into the cause of freedom." The army had few trained doctors or nurses, all of which were male. Wounded soldiers received poor care. After the first few battles, it became clear just how much they needed better care. Women demanded to be allowed to help, especially with the nursing. The army was against employing women nurses at the start. However, the urgent need for help made the army give in.

The Blackwells called a meeting at the infirmary to talk about how best to train nurses to help wounded soldiers. Other women were calling small meetings to organize making bandages and other items for the wounded. The notice about the Blackwells' meeting was accidentally published in *The New York Times*. Hundreds of women showed up, too many to fit into the infirmary. About four thousand women came to the next meeting, which was held in a larger hall only two weeks after the war began. They set up an organization called the Woman's Central Association of Relief for the Sick and Wounded of the Army.

Blackwell knew about the British Sanitary Commission that had helped the British army during the Crimean War. The British army had faced similar problems with unsanitary conditions allowing disease to spread among the soldiers. Together with other women from the central association, Blackwell set about forming a sanitary commission to help the Union army. No government officials were interested in the women's plan, but some men thought it was a great idea. Led by Unitarian minister

War and Disease

During the Civil War, a soldier might be killed on the battlefield or die from a wound. However, it was much more likely that he would die from an infectious disease. Many of the men hadn't had childhood diseases, such as measles and chicken pox, which spread and killed many adults. Water and food supplies were often dirty. There were poor, if any, toilets and drains. Together, these conditions allowed diseases such as dysentery and typhoid to take hold easily. Hospital conditions were so bad they also spread diseases. Doctors did too as they tended patient after patient without washing their hands in between. More than 400,000 soldiers died from disease during the war, or about one out of every ten fighting men.

Dr. Henry Bellows, a group of male doctors traveled to Washington, D.C., to persuade President Lincoln to allow the women to help in May 1861. They felt that men could show the government how important the women's aid group could be.

On June 13, President Lincoln was finally convinced and set up the United States Sanitary Commission. Bellows was named president, and other men filled most of the top positions. The army didn't believe that it was responsible for the health and morale of its soldiers. The U.S. Sanitary Commission tried to take that responsibility. It provided nurses, cooks, medicine, hospitals, ambulances, and transport ships. It checked the camps and hospitals, advising those who ran them on how to make them more hygienic. It also collected and distributed canned food that was clean and safe to eat. Warm clothing was made and sent, and temporary shelters were set up to house soldiers as they traveled. Volunteers gave soldiers writing paper and stamps or wrote letters home for those who couldn't.

Some of the men involved in the sanitary commission didn't want Elizabeth Blackwell to be in charge of organizing the nurses. They agreed to give that job to Dorothea Dix. She was not a doctor or a nurse but was a well-known campaigner for reforming insane asylums. The Blackwells thought Dix was a great woman, full of charity and kindness, but not a very good organizer.

Dix sent the trained nurses to the army hospitals and battlefields, but others organized their training. In New York, the Blackwells met the potential nurses, decided who was capable, and then trained them. Elizabeth Blackwell gave nine lectures to the trainees on subjects such as wound care and hygiene. The trainees also spent a month working at Bellevue Hospital in New York, learning practical nursing. Then, armed with this basic knowledge and some gear, they went to do their best to help. Elizabeth wrote about one nurse they trained who she had thought "feeble-looking." This nurse surprised her by wading through the blood on the battlefield for two days and nights after the Battle of Gettysburg, heroically helping fallen soldiers.

By 1863, there were more than seven thousand sanitary commission groups in the North. Tens of thousands of volunteers, mostly women, and thousands of paid workers did important jobs to keep the army going. As well as some government money, the U.S. Sanitary Commission relied on holding bazaars to fund its work. By the end of the war, these sanitary fairs had raised about $6 million.

WARTIME AT THE INFIRMARY

While helping the sanitary commission as much as they could, the Blackwells also kept the infirmary going strong during the Civil War.

The Blackwells helped prepare nurses to treat soldiers wounded in battle.

The number of patients treated grew to about seven thousand a year by the end of the war. For the most part, their work continued as before, teaching students, training graduates and nurses, and caring for women and children. Some of their patients were former slaves who had escaped to the North and to freedom.

At the beginning of the Civil War, many people in the North fought to keep the United States together. Most Northerners agreed with the war. Cheerful volunteers filled the army. They went into the first battles sure they would win quickly. As time went on, and the war proved difficult to win, people grew worried. Families were losing fathers, husbands, and sons to the bloody battles. In January 1863, President Lincoln made the Emancipation Proclamation that freed all the slaves held in the Confederate territories. The Civil War was now truly about slavery, not about keeping the Union together.

More and more former slaves headed north to freedom. Some enlisted in the Union army, and others looked for work in the North.

Civil War Nurses

More than three thousand women worked as paid nurses during the Civil War. They were some of the first organized nurses in the United States. They wanted to do real, satisfying work instead of watch the war overrun their lives. They saw the worst war wounds and diseases. The nurses made a real difference to the soldiers they cared for. As well as saving lives and giving hope, they helped women gain respect in the military. By the end of the Civil War, the army required one-third of its hospital nurses to be women.

Tensions grew in the North between blacks and whites. Many white people feared losing their jobs to black people, who were often willing to work for lower wages.

In March 1863, Congress passed the Enrollment Act that said all men aged twenty to forty-five would be drafted into the Union army. A drafted man could hire someone to take his place or he could buy his way out of the draft for $300. This was a whole year's earnings for a poor man. The act took effect on July 11. People were angry because they had to fight for black freedom and because only rich men could get out of performing the service. Afraid they might die, some white people started rioting. On July 13, riots broke out in New York City.

Elizabeth and Kitty were in New Jersey when the riots began. They went across the river to New York and headed for the infirmary on foot. Rioters had pulled down the telegraph lines. People had closed and shuttered their homes and stores. Mobs of armed angry white men searched the streets for any black people they could find. When Elizabeth

The orphanage for African American children was one of the many places destroyed during the riots.

and Kitty reached the infirmary, they found people panicking. There were black women patients, some awaiting the birth of their babies. Some of the white patients wanted them thrown out in case they all got killed because they were housing them.

Blackwell refused to send anyone out into the streets. She and the other staff worked hard to keep the patients calm, even covering their eyes so they wouldn't see the flames outside. A black woman gave birth to her child on the first night of the riots. Three days passed before the rioting ended, but the infirmary was not touched.

About 120 black people were killed during the riots, and many more were hurt. They were stoned, shot, or hanged. The Colored Orphan Asylum, where eight hundred black children lived, was set on fire and burned to the ground. Buildings were looted, and bricks thrown through windows. About $2 million worth of damage was done.

THE WAR ENDS

In June 1864, Elizabeth Blackwell was invited to Washington, D.C., to visit the Nursing Corps. She met with President Lincoln and talked about the war. She thought he was friendly and appreciated that he took her seriously.

By the end of January 1865, Congress had approved the Thirteenth Amendment abolishing slavery. President Lincoln had made many enemies, and one of them shot him on April 14, 1865. Blackwell was very sad when he died because she thought he was a hero and a kind man as well. During April, the South surrendered, and the war was over by May 1865.

President Abraham Lincoln was assassinated shortly before the end of the Civil War.

After the war was over, life was different for women. Women were common in the medical profession, and many were fired up by their experiences as wartime nurses. The Blackwells felt that women were becoming accepted as doctors but that there still weren't enough spots in medical colleges for them. They decided the time had come to open their own women's medical college attached to the infirmary. Elizabeth wrote, "We took this step, however, with hesitation, for our own feeling was adverse to the formation of an entirely separate school for women."

In 1865, the infirmary applied for permission to open a medical school and began to raise money to fund it. In November 1868, the Women's Medical College of the New York Infirmary opened. Elizabeth gave a speech about how doctors must have a great deal of knowledge in order to diagnose and treat patients. The best physicians would also have sympathy for their patients. The college was to have a new philosophy, different from that of other medical schools. Students would attend for three years instead of two. They would have hands-on lessons and would have to talk about their work with their teachers.

The Bloodiest War

During the four years of the Civil War, about three million men fought. Of these, 620,000 died, and 50,000 went home missing an arm or leg. Many battles saw terrible casualties. In April 1862, 13,000 Union and 10,000 Confederate soldiers were killed or wounded at the Battle of Shiloh. This was more casualties than in all the American wars before combined. On September 17, 1862, the Battle of Antietam was the bloodiest day in U.S. history. More than 26,000 men were killed, wounded, or missing. At Cold Harbor in June 1863, seven thousand Union soldiers were killed or wounded in just twenty minutes. Lincoln's famous Gettysburg Address was given at a ceremony dedicating a national cemetery at the battlefield because so many had died there.

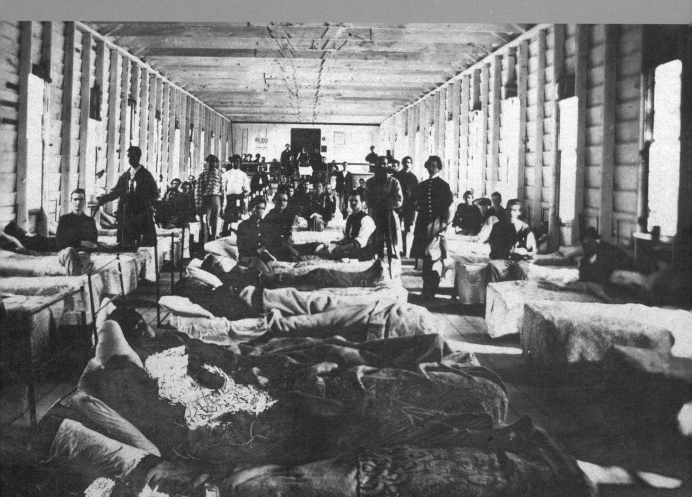

Elizabeth would be the first professor of hygiene ever, giving hygiene equal importance along with the other subjects students learned. Elizabeth thought hygiene was more important than ever. She wrote, "It has always seemed to me . . . that the first and constant aim of

A historical illustration shows the anatomy lecture room at the Woman's Medical College of the New York Infirmary.

the family physician should be to [give] . . . the sanitary knowledge that would enable parents to bring up healthy children." Emily was the professor of obstetrics and women's diseases. Lucy Abbott taught midwifery. The other five teachers were men. The first class had about seventeen women students in it, including Sophia Jex-Blake from England.

Soon there were changes. Instead of the staff giving students a final examination, a special examination board with none of the college's own staff on it was formed. The questions asked were harder than the ones most other medical schools asked, because the Blackwells wanted to produce the best-qualified doctors ever. The length of the training course was increased to four years. Both medical experts and the general public saw that the Women's Medical College was an excellent school.

The biggest change was that Elizabeth decided it was time to return to England for good. She wrote, "In 1869 the early pioneer work in America was ended." The challenge of helping women enter medicine still awaited her in England. On July 15, 1869, Elizabeth and Kitty set sail. Emily stayed behind to develop the college and run the infirmary. Emily decided that she didn't want to leave medicine after all and was a great physician and administrator until she retired. The Women's Medical College stayed open until 1899, when Cornell University Medical College agreed to give both men and women an equal education. All the students at the Women's Medical College transferred to Cornell, and Emily closed the school.

EIGHT

Starting Over

Elizabeth Blackwell arrived in England feeling physically worn out. She wanted a rest. She took Kitty to the Lake District for a vacation. They then went to Bristol for the Social Science Congress in September 1869. There were discussions on topics such as education, health, trade, and helping the poor. Blackwell spoke on educating women doctors.

A session on the Contagious Diseases Acts was closed to women. Because she was a doctor, Blackwell was allowed to attend. Under the acts, prostitutes were required to be licensed. Women who were thought to be prostitutes were checked for diseases, to help stop diseases from spreading. The men using prostitutes, on the other hand, were not to be touched. Blackwell and many others thought the acts were unfair and made prostitution acceptable. Getting the acts repealed became her next great "campaign against the unequal standard of sexual morality."

Since she had been a medical student at the Blockley Almshouse, the "selfish relations of men and women" had troubled Blackwell. She met women suffering after having been raped. She saw prostitutes suffering from sexually transmitted diseases. These things outraged Blackwell. She said, "I will not be blind, indifferent, or stupid in relation to this matter, as are most women." She felt very strongly that holding men to one standard and women to another did neither any good. Blackwell thought men and women should have the chance to respect each other's minds and bodies. Then they could develop noble and beautiful relationships, which would make society better. Blackwell thought that "the world can never be redeemed till this central relation of life is placed on a truer footing."

Blackwell lectured, wrote, and taught her message about sex. She said sex was a basic, natural function of human beings. If parents educated their children about their bodies and taught them self-restraint and self-respect, children would grow into healthy adults. If children saw examples all around them of women being treated badly or differently according to their class, they would grow up knowing only that double standard. The key was to show all women the same respect, whether they were servants or royalty.

Blackwell thought the way to change society was by changing the laws that governed it. She worked for the next seventeen years on getting rid of the Contagious Diseases Acts. She succeeded. The acts were repealed in 1886. Blackwell thought that educating the people was another valuable tool. Already, Blackwell had focused on hygiene as part of her lifelong quest to educate women about their bodies. Now she grew even more specific. She wanted mothers to have more information about sex and morality so they could raise their children to have knowledge and power. She had always believed that women, and especially mothers, held the key to change through their families.

LIFE IN ENGLAND

While at the Social Science Congress in Bristol, Blackwell visited the house on Wilson Street where she had lived as a young child. It was a happy visit that brought back memories. She wrote about "the home which I remembered as so large, but which then looked so small." She vividly remembered being forbidden to attend a dinner party after being naughty as a child. She also had a vision of her father coming home, turning his key in the lock, and walking into the hall in a white flannel suit. This realistic, clear vision startled her.

Blackwell had been a religious person her whole life. From her experience as a dissident Congregationalist, Blackwell made social and moral reform a part of her religion, as it had been for her parents. She changed churches, becoming a Unitarian for a while. Whatever church she belonged to, she felt strongly that being Christian made her morally responsible to push the reforms she supported. She wrote that from 1869, "During the following twenty years the responsibility of the Christian physician assumed to me an ever-deepening significance."

Blackwell worked with incredible energy. She threw herself into three main activities: setting up a private practice, working to repeal the Contagious Diseases Acts, and working to get women into careers in

Francis Power Cobbe was a leading animal rights activist in her day.

medicine. In 1870, she set up her practice in London, and started seeing many patients. She lived for a while with her old friend, Barbara Leigh Smith. By that point, Barbara had married and was named Madame Bodichon. Blackwell's social life began to whirl as she met some of the top thinkers and artists of the day. Dante Gabriel Rossetti, George Eliot, and Robert Browning were guests in the house. Other guests were political reformers. Blackwell enjoyed the free exchange of ideas that kept her thinking and learning.

Blackwell was becoming less happy with the common practice of testing medicines and scientific theories on animals. She wrote, "I have long since realised that conscience and humanity must guide intellectual activity and curiosity, or we wander from the high-road of truth into a labyrinth of error." She felt that testing on animals was immoral and cruel. One of her books, *Medicine and Morality*, explored this idea. Blackwell wrote, "There are limits to scientific investigation; knowledge is not its own justification." One of the people she met at Madame Bodichon's was Frances Power

Cobbe, a leading animal-rights campaigner. They became friends and talked about morality and animal testing.

WOMEN AND EDUCATION

Blackwell worked to get women accepted into medical schools. In Britain, she helped campaign for a law allowing women have equal rights before medical examining boards. This meant women would be able to study medicine and then qualify as doctors. Elizabeth Garrett, then named Elizabeth Garrett Anderson, had become the second woman on the British Medical Register in 1866. Blackwell also worked with Garrett Anderson and Sophia Jex-Blake to plan a women's hospital and school in London. They were still raising money for it as well.

Blackwell was part of another movement to help women get an equal footing with men. Although she disagreed with some of the things women's rights campaigners said, she agreed that women should be allowed to vote. Around the world women's struggle to get the vote had been long and hard. In Britain many women went to jail and even lost their lives for the cause. Unmarried women who owned homes were allowed to vote in local elections from 1869. In 1918, all women over the age of thirty were finally given the right to vote in all elections. Elizabeth was the first Blackwell woman to cast her own vote, in a local British election in 1870.

In 1870, Blackwell gave another of her lectures on hygiene called "How to Keep a Household in Health." A newspaper published an article about her talk, stating that it was shocking and awful. Nevertheless, Blackwell was thronged with letters asking for advice after the article came out. She refused to answer them, saying a doctor needed to be consulted in person. People clearly wanted this education, as the large number of letters showed. In February 1871, she gave another lecture called "On the Religion of Health." Nothing unusual happened after that one. Both lectures were directed toward average people so they could learn about how important it was to prevent disease. Blackwell felt more and more that preventing illness was better than trying to cure illness.

Theories on Germs

In 1849, William Budd and John Snow said that cholera came from bacteria found in water, but most people didn't believe them. Louis Pasteur published his germ theory in 1861, saying that tiny germs only visible through a microscope caused disease and suffering. Not enough people had microscopes to see and believe for themselves, so the theory was not widely accepted. In the late 1860s, Joseph Lister started performing antiseptic surgery in English hospitals, which meant sterilizing hands, instruments, and wounds. During the 1870s, antiseptic surgery became widespread, because it caused death rates from surgery to go down dramatically. It wasn't until 1890 that the germ theory was finally accepted. People then knew how important it was to prevent the spread of germs.

NINE

London Triumph

In 1871, Elizabeth Blackwell began a new group called the National Health Society in London. Its motto was "prevention is better than cure." The founders were men and women, doctors and others concerned about hygiene and education. The society intended to spread "sanitary knowledge among all the people." Members gave inexpensive lectures and published pamphlets. They covered topics such as diet, hygiene, "prevention of epidemic disease," and "effects of modern dress on health." The society hoped to educate many women from all classes. These women would then spread the information among their families, friends, and servants, and the health of the whole nation would be improved.

Although it wasn't full medical education, the National Health Society did offer medical training courses for women. At the end of the courses, they had to pass exams. They didn't get degrees, but they did get certificates and solid knowledge. Women could study topics such as ambulance work, childcare, nursing, and home health.

Blackwell and other members of the society, such as Edwin Chadwick and Dr. William Hardwicke, were concerned about the state of housing for working-class people. They feared that until the standards that everyone lived under were raised, too many people would die early. The National Health Society worked with the government to improve living standards. People didn't have enough places to exercise outdoors in cities, so it got school playgrounds opened up after school hours so people could exercise there. Even though people understood by that point how important clean drinking water was, many people still had no access to it. The National Health Society worked to make clean water available to everyone.

Blackwell had introduced the sanitary visitor's job to the New York Infirmary. Now the National Health Society started a similar plan to train health visitors. These women mostly went to the homes of poor

Health Visitors

Today, more than ten thousand health visitors look after the "health of the whole community" in Britain. They are all nurses with extra training in education. Health visitors help people stay well. They give people practical advice and also listen to their worries. Every family with young children has a health visitor. He or she visits their homes and sees the children for regular health checks. Other health visitors see elderly people or deal with different medical issues.

people. They checked people's overall health and living standards. They helped educate them in better hygiene. By 1900, the National Health Society offered a course for health visitors that awarded a diploma. In 1920, the government decided to make the National Health Society part of the Board of Education. It ran an official training school specifically for training health visitors. It kept up its important work until 1947. Then it broke up, and the National Health Service took over running the medical services for the whole country, including health visitors.

ILLNESS STRIKES

In 1872, Blackwell was working hard but found time to pursue another interest. She had always been interested in the way communities lived together. Blackwell had a wide range of experiences with many kinds of housing, from wealthy homes with large grounds to tenements crowded to bursting with poor families. She wanted people to be able to live in a healthy and clean way. She was also concerned about people's moral and emotional lives. Society as she had experienced it had many problems. She thought helping people feel more equal and asking them to work together in a community might be successful. This is called cooperative living.

Blackwell heard of a cooperative group in France that she wanted to visit. It was a long trip, and she was worn out by it. This group had set up its own factories, schools, meeting places, and homes. It supported itself by making stoves. The visit was interesting, but "intense." When Blackwell returned to London, she got very ill. She was suffering from biliary colic. This is a kind of pain in the stomach and gut. It can be very severe and last for a long time. Blackwell saw doctors and tried to cure herself but only grew worse. In 1873, she had to give up her practice in London. She traveled to warmer places such as Rome to try and recover.

Blackwell had helped Elizabeth Garrett Anderson while she was running her dispensary in London. In 1872, the dispensary was renamed the New Hospital for Women. It grew over the years. Patients were always given the choice of seeing women doctors. When Garrett Anderson died in 1917, it was renamed the Elizabeth Garrett Anderson Hospital. It is now part of the University College London Hospitals.

After facing many difficulties in getting medical degrees, a small group of women got the money together to set up their own medical school. Sophia Jex-Blake had not been allowed to keep studying medicine at Edinburgh University in Scotland, so she led the group. In 1874, Sophia Jex-Blake and Elizabeth Garrett Anderson finally opened the London School of Medicine for Women. Some male doctors agreed to teach the

Elizabeth Garrett Anderson

Born in London in 1836, Elizabeth Garrett was one of twelve children. Her father was wealthy enough to educate the girls as well as the boys. He supported her when she decided to become a doctor. She couldn't get into medical school in England, even after she became an apothecary and set up her own dispensary in 1866. She had to learn French and attend the University of Paris to get her M.D. In 1871, she married James Anderson, a businessman. She had three children. After retiring from medicine in 1902, she became the first female mayor in England. Garrett Anderson died in 1917.

women. Blackwell had raised money and helped plan the new school. When she was offered the job of teaching midwifery, or the process of delivering babies, she couldn't turn it down. She went back to London and started teaching. Sadly, her illness grew worse. She finished teaching the course but decided she had to give up living in London for good.

Students from the London School of Medicine for Women needed a hospital in which to gain practical experience. The New Hospital for Women offered some places, but it was small. In 1877, the Royal Free Hospital let the women students work there. In that same year, Sophia Jex-Blake and four other women were added to the British Medical Register. Forty years after the London School opened, six hundred of the one thousand women on the British Medical Register were its graduates. In 1898, the school and hospital were renamed the London (Royal Free Hospital) School of Medicine for Women. It was the only women's

The Royal Free Hospital was one of the few places that allowed female medical students to gain practical experience.

medical school in England until 1947, when it allowed men to enroll. It is still open today and is now called the Royal Free and University College Medical School.

LEAVING LONDON

Blackwell felt sad about leaving London. She wasn't sure what to do with the rest of her life, because she felt unable to lecture or have a private practice. She had won the battle to set up a school and hospital for women. In 1876, the British government passed a law forcing the different medical licensing groups to allow women take their exams, so another victory was won.

Never still for long, Blackwell traveled to warm places such as the south of France. She concentrated on getting better. When she felt stronger, Blackwell started writing a great deal. She was upset that she didn't feel well enough to practice as a doctor again. However, she decided that she would keep learning about the things that interested her. She would help others by writing about the things she found important. Blackwell felt strongly that ". . . our medical profession has not yet fully realised the special and weighty responsibility which rest upon it to watch over the cradle of the race; to see that human beings are well born, well nourished, and well educated." Many of her writings are about reaching this goal. Some are meant for other doctors, and some for parents and teachers.

Blackwell's first published writing, her thesis on typhus at Blockley, was published in 1849 in the *Buffalo Medical Journal*. In the following fifty years, Blackwell wrote many articles, pamphlets, and books. They were about moral and sex education, medical morality, and her life story. Some people think her autobiography *Pioneer Work in Opening the Medical Profession to Women*, published in 1895, to be her greatest book.

Some think Blackwell's best book is her *Counsel to Parents on the Moral Education of Their Children*. This book took two years to get published because the subject matter was considered so scandalous. At a time when it was still shocking to talk about bodies, it discussed sex education. It came out in 1878. In it she wrote,

> The whole structure of society must depend upon the character of [the family], and the powers that can be unfolded from it. Morality in sex will be found to be the essence of all morality, securing principles of justice, honour, and uprightness. . . . Women, as well as men, create society. Their share is not a silent one . . . it is often overlooked, misunderstood, or despised. Nevertheless it is of vital importance.

In this book, Blackwell tells parents to raise their children morally, with equality shown to men and women. She also advises practical things, like keeping clean, getting physical exercise and fresh air, and letting boys and girls get to know each other as people to get rid of any unhealthy sense of mystery between them. She speaks out against prostitution. She also says that children should learn about sex from reliable sources such as parents, teachers, or doctors, not from gossip and rumors.

Elizabeth Blackwell, excluding a few trips, spent the rest of her life in Hastings.

Active Until the End

In 1879, Elizabeth Blackwell and Kitty moved to Hastings, on the southern coast of England. They lived in a house called Rock House, set on a hill overlooking the English Channel. This was to be Blackwell's final move.

Blackwell was still interested in social reform. She felt it was wrong to think "that because forms of evil have always existed in society, therefore they must always exist." Anything that would make the world a better place to live in grabbed her attention. She kept learning about cooperative living. She looked into how cities could be improved. She was concerned with the way prisons were run. She wanted women to have access to many kinds of education in technical and scientific fields. All of these topics worked together with her medical and moral interests.

Elizabeth Blackwell wanted men and women to have equal chances and everyone to live healthy, productive, happy lives.

Blackwell felt that she had a special duty to keep reminding other doctors that a true understanding of health came from seeing how a person lived his or her life, and then helping improve the overall picture.

Women as Doctors

YEAR	NUMBER OF WOMEN M.D.S IN THE UNITED STATES
1852	30
1858	300
1880	2432
1900	7387
1910	7399

YEAR	WOMEN AS A PERCENTAGE OF ALL DOCTORS IN THE UNITED STATES
1914	10%
1924	6%
1970	7.8%
1975	9.1%
1980	11.6%
1997	22%

She believed that doctors and scientists had a moral duty to treat the whole person, not just his or her disease. She knew that germs caused disease. However, Blackwell doubted that all the fuss over germs was a good thing. She thought that people would want to only get rid of the germs and forget about all the other causes of disease that needed attention. The bigger picture of hygiene, lifestyle, living conditions, food, and exercise might be lost because the focus on disease.

The focus on germs is one of the reasons she was against vaccination. A vaccine is basically a small bit of a germ that would make the person sick in a greater quantity. Blackwell believed that putting a bit of disease into a person could cause more harm than good.

Scientists had to remember their moral boundaries in their research and do nothing that would make people less sensitive to suffering, such as testing on animals. Blackwell thought that women doctors would help keep this moral light shining. She was upset when women who became doctors followed what she saw as the male way of doing things. She wrote, "I recognise that our women physicians do not all and always see the glorious moral mission, which as women physicians they are called on to fulfill."

LAST TRAVELS

At the age of eighty-one, Blackwell took Kitty to Bristol for the last time. She was upset by how much it had all changed. At eighty-six, in 1906, Blackwell sailed for the United States. She had been away for thirty-seven years, but it was now Emily's eightieth birthday. Five of her sisters and brothers had died, but many nieces and nephews were

gathering with the remaining ones for a party. Two of Blackwell's nieces were also doctors by that point. Emily had also adopted a daughter. Her daughter and grandchildren kept her happy at the end of her life. Although Elizabeth enjoyed the four-month trip, she was too ill while in the United States to visit the New York Infirmary.

Blackwell and Kitty spent many summers in Kilmun, Scotland. Blackwell was very happy there, staying in a small hotel on the edge of Holy Loch. She enjoyed the clean, healthy air and loved walking in the countryside. In 1907, while visiting Kilmun, Blackwell fell down the hotel stairs. She hadn't broken any bones, but the shock of the fall hurt her spirit. Kitty wrote that she "lost some of her powers of concentration" after that fall. She did no more work, but remained cheerful. By 1909, she was not aware of much around her and didn't understand when she was told that her brother Henry had died.

On May 31, 1910, Elizabeth Blackwell died in Hastings. She faced no specific illnesses or diseases at the end, but instead died peacefully of old age. She was eighty-nine. After a funeral in St. Clement's Church in

Hastings on June 4, her body was taken to Scotland. She was buried in the churchyard at Kilmun the next day. Her local friends and people from the college she did some work with in Glasgow came to the simple service in the parish church. A large Celtic cross stands on her grave.

TRIBUTES AND HONORS

After Blackwell died, Kitty Barry changed her last name to Blackwell to honor her "Doctor." Many other honors were given to Elizabeth Blackwell. In 1970, the U.S. Postal Service issued a stamp with Blackwell's portrait on it. There are plaques and portraits in many of the places she lived and worked in the United States and Britain. At Rock House in Hastings, there is a tribute to her. It was written by Robert Browning and changed for her:

One who never turned her back but marched breast forward,
Never doubted clouds would break,

There have been many awards and tributes marking Elizabeth Blackwell's pioneering spirit. This is the U.S. postal stamp issued in her honor.

Never dreamed, though rights were worsted, wrong would triumph,
Held we fall to rise, are baffled to fight better,
Sleep to wake.

Before she died, the William Smith College for Women opened as part of what was formerly Geneva Medical College, then called Hobart College. William Smith College named its first dormitory for women after Elizabeth Blackwell and asked Emily Blackwell and Alice Stone Blackwell to come to the ceremony to dedicate it.

In 1958, Hobart and William Smith Colleges gave the first Elizabeth Blackwell Award. It is given to a woman who has performed outstanding service to humankind. The award includes a sculpture of Elizabeth

Medical Societies

As well as facing the problems of getting educated and qualified, women had to be admitted to different medical societies to get true recognition in the field. Many people thought women were unfit to be doctors or feared they would reduce male doctors' earnings. In 1847, the American Medical Association was founded, but it didn't let women in until 1915. California was the first state to allow women into its medical society in 1853. Pennsylvania was the last in 1915. The Royal College of Physicians of London admitted women in 1909. The Royal College of Physicians and Surgeons of Glasgow allowed women to become members in 1912.

OFFICIAL FIRST DAY COVER

*Hobart &
William Smith
Colleges*

GENEVA MEDICAL COLLEGE

Honoring

Elizabeth Blackwell, M.D.
1821–1910
FIRST WOMAN M.D. IN AMERICA
GRADUATED JANUARY 23, 1849

Art Craft

Elizabeth Blackwell was a trailblazer who opened up the medical field for all the women doctors that followed her.

Blackwell. Many celebrated women have received the award, including Madeleine K. Albright, Billie Jean King, Wilma Mankiller, and Sandra Day O'Connor. There is also a New York Infirmary Annual Award for a woman doctor who has done outstanding work in medicine.

Perhaps the best tribute to her work comes from Blackwell's own writings. As the London *Times* said in her obituary, she was a true pioneer. She blazed a trail and then helped other people to follow it. At the end of her life Elizabeth Blackwell wrote, "No one who was not alive sixty years ago can realise the iron wall hemming in on every side any young women who wished to earn her living or to do anything outside of the narrowest conventional groove. Such a woman was simply crushed. Those who were of a character not to be crushed without resistance, had to fight for their lives, and their fight broke the way through for the others to follow."

Timeline

1854 The dispensary is incorporated as the New York Dispensary for Poor Women and Children in January. In October, Blackwell adopts Kitty Barry.

1857 The New York Infirmary for Indigent Women and Children opens on May 12.
1859 Blackwell becomes the first woman on the British Medical Register. She works to get medical education and special hospitals for women in England.

1861 Civil War begins.

Blackwell helps found the United States Sanitary Commission.

1865 President Lincoln is assassinated in April. Later the Civil War ends.

1866 Elizabeth Garrett becomes the second woman on British Medical Register.

1868 Women's Medical College of the New York Infirmary opens with Elizabeth and Emily Blackwell as two of the professors.

1869 Blackwell moves to England and works to end the Contagious Diseases Acts.

1870 Blackwell opens a private practice in London.

1871 Blackwell helps found the National Health Society in England.

1873 Blackwell gives up private practice because of her poor health.

1874 London School of Medicine for Women opens. Blackwell becomes lecturer in midwifery.

1876 British law makes medical licensing groups offer exams to women.

1877 In December, Blackwell resigns from the London School of Medicine for Women.

1878 Blackwell privately prints *Counsel to Parents on the Moral Education of Their Children*.

1879 Blackwell and Kitty move to Rock House in Hastings.

1886 The Contagious Diseases Acts are repealed.

1895 Blackwell publishes her autobiography *Pioneer Work in Opening the Medical Profession to Women*.

1899 Women's Medical College of the New York Infirmary closes, and all students are transferred to Cornell University Medical College.

1910 Elizabeth Blackwell dies in Hastings on May 31. She is buried in Kilmun, Scotland.

To Find Out More

BOOKS

Glimm, Adele, *Elizabeth Blackwell: First Woman Doctor of Modern Times*. New York: McGraw-Hill, 2000.

Henry, Joanne Landers, *Elizabeth Blackwell, Girl Doctor*. New York: Aladdin Paperbacks, 1996.

Kline, Nancy, *Elizabeth Blackwell: A Doctor's Triumph*. Berkeley, CA: Conari Press, 1997.

ORGANIZATIONS AND ONLINE SITES

Elizabeth Blackwell, M.D.
http://campus.hws.edu/his/blackwell

This is the Web site put together by Hobart and William Smith Colleges, where Elizabeth Blackwell went to medical school when it was still called Geneva College. It is packed with resources, including many historic articles and good biographical information.

Elizabeth Blackwell Online Exhibit
http://www.nlm.nih.gov/hmd/blackwell/index.html

This is the online version of an exhibit about Elizabeth Blackwell from the National Library of Medicine in Maryland.

Gale Group: Elizabeth Blackwell
http://www.gale.com/free_resources/whm/bio/blackwell_e.htm

This is a summary of the times Blackwell lived in, with useful timelines, and a biography of Blackwell.

People Doing Science: Elizabeth Blackwell
http://science-education.nih.gov/snapshots.nsf/story?openform&pds~
Elizabeth_Blackwell_Doctor

This is a nice, short biography, with the factual error that she was only accepted at Geneva Medical College.

Women's History: Elizabeth Blackwell
http://womenshistory.about.com/library/bio/blbio_blackwell_eliz.htm

This is one article from a series of Web pages on women's history. You can find out about many of the issues facing women in Blackwell's time on this site.

A Note on Sources

Elizabeth Blackwell wrote many books during her life. You can find copies of some of them with the help of your local librarian. Some are difficult to read, since they were written for other doctors. Others are very interesting to read, especially her autobiography, *Pioneer Work in Opening the Medical Profession to Women*. She tells the story of her groundbreaking work as she looks back on her life, and gives you parts of her diaries and letters to read. Other people have written about Blackwell's life, but nothing else gives you as clear an account of her feelings as she lived it. I enjoyed reading it and felt moved by her words.

Blackwell and her relatives wrote thousands of pages of letters and diaries. Many of these are collected in the Library of Congress. You can see what is there at their Web site. There are about 29,000 items in this collection!

If reading about Blackwell's life has made you interested in the struggle for women's rights, early women's work in new fields, or medical history, there are hundreds of places for you to keep learning. You can ask your teacher or librarian to help you find out more. You can do your own research as well about how people you know have made choices about their lives, and about how getting into different jobs has changed over time. Try talking to your family doctor about how he or she became a doctor, and asking adults you know about how they chose their careers.

—*Tristan Boyer Binns*

Index

About the Author

Tristan Boyer Binns has an English degree from Tufts University. She has written twenty-five books for children and young adults on subjects from the American flag to hermit crabs to the CIA. She has taught creative writing to children and adults, and run writing workshops. Before beginning her writing career, Tristan was Publishing Director for an international library book publisher. Researching people's lives and the history of daily life is a real joy for her.